MASTERPIECES IN COLOR

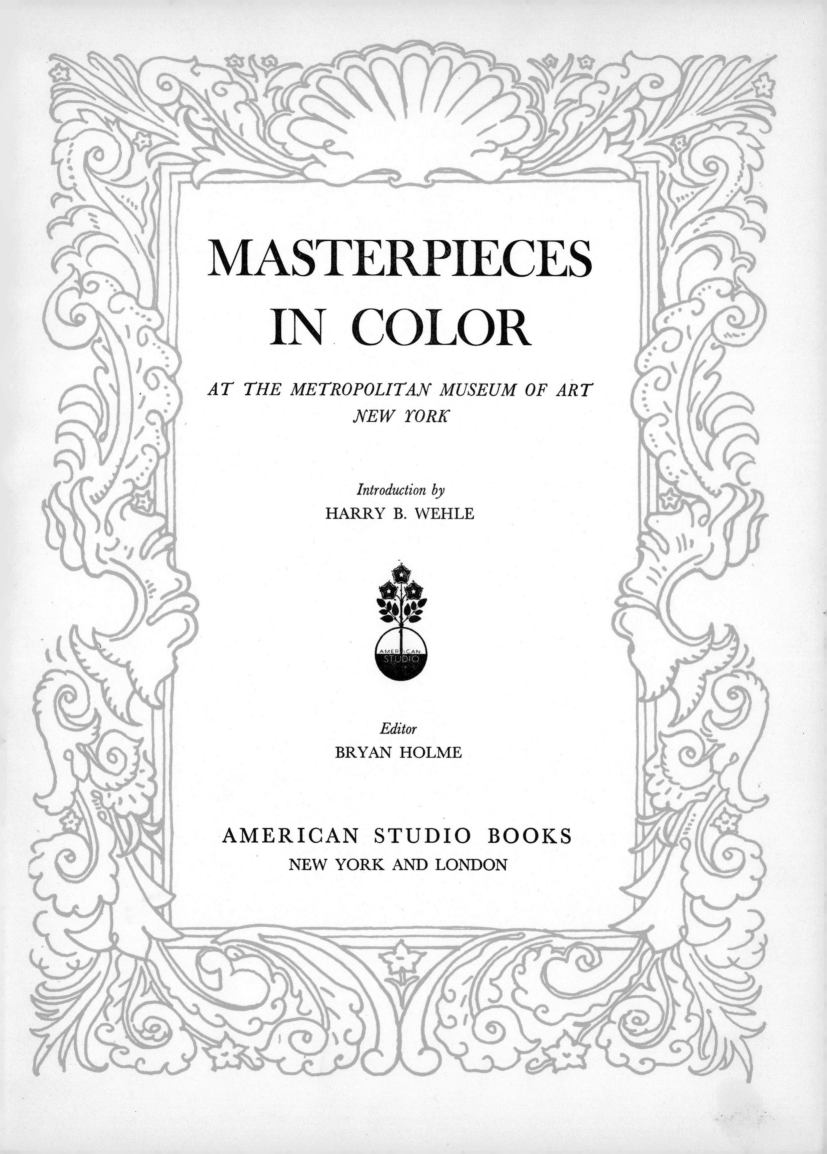

MASTERPIECES IN COLOR

AT THE METROPOLITAN MUSEUM OF ART
NEW YORK

Introduction by
HARRY B. WEHLE

Editor
BRYAN HOLME

AMERICAN STUDIO BOOKS
NEW YORK AND LONDON

ACKNOWLEDGMENTS

It is hard adequately to express our gratitude to the directorate and staff of the Metropolitan Museum of Art for their great encouragement in producing this book of color reproductions. We would especially like to thank Mr. Horace H. F. Jayne, Vice Director, and Mr. J. Frederick Olsen, Supervisor of Printing, for their untiring energy and assistance. We are also indebted to "The Art News" and Simon & Schuster for courtesies extended on plates of their ownership and to Mr. Sam Faber, Colorist.

Notes in the Museum's monthly Bulletins provide the basis for the descriptive material used in the Introduction.

Printed in the United States of America by the Plantin Press, New York City, N. Y.

FOREWORD

Each individual interested in paintings must have his own reaction to the color plates which reproduce them. Lacking, as they still do, absolute fidelity in matters of color, texture, and scale, such reproductions almost necessarily give varying degrees of satisfaction to different beholders. To a very particular few the inaccuracies constitute a complete bar to enjoyment. To many others the prints serve as helpful reminders of originals which they know quite well at first hand but are unable to remember once they are beyond eyeshot. For this class of persons, and it is a numerous class, the color reproduction even at this stage of its technical development is far more accurate than the memories carried away. A third class, to whom color reproductions can mean a great deal, is composed of people who are not so fortunately situated that they can often visit the places where fine original paintings may be enjoyed, and for them the color print may become a primary source of satisfaction.

The Metropolitan Museum of Art over a span of years has been adding to its fund of color plates based on objects in its collections. Some of these plates are better than others, and the accretion has been slow. In the past few years the pace has quickened and in many cases the quality too is higher. The Museum's Bulletins carry color prints on their covers, often representing details of paintings rather than entire works, for thus the reduction in scale may be obviated or at least need not be so drastic. Recent wartime restrictions have proved to be a distressingly limiting factor. Manpower and materials have also been scarce here as in other non-military enterprises. Thus one of the Museum's cherished projects has lain for a time in comparative abeyance, namely the project of building up a full reservoir of color plates reproducing all its most important works of art.

Meanwhile, a fuller utilization of the plates already at hand in the Museum, in addition to those that have been made outside, has been brought into effect in this firstbook of reproductions in color, chosen by the publishers. The direction taken is unquestionably an excellent one and the Museum is glad that a beginning is made in the task of getting to a wider public reproductions in color of its treasures.

HARRY B. WEHLE
Curator of Paintings in the
Metropolitan Museum of Art

INTRODUCTION

WITH the first of a selection of famous paintings at the Metropolitan Museum of Art, we enter the golden age of Renaissance painting in Italy. Sassetta's "The Journey of the Magi" shows us the regal cavalcade winding its way down the pebbly road between gray hills, leaving behind it the rosy gates of a mediaeval city. The sky, through which a file of wild cranes flies, is aglow with early morning light. A huge golden star hangs low against the pallid near-by rocks; then come riding the three Kings, one old and bearded, the others young and gay. These in turn are followed by a jester and divers courtiers. Never, perhaps, has the old tale been told with a greater measure of naive charm.

"The Presentation in the Temple" (*Plate II*) is characteristic of Giovanni di Paolo's elaborated style. On this small panel the much loved Sienese artist exhibits to the full his dainty, somewhat high strung vivacity, his delight in slender graceful *dramatis personae*, with strange thin faces and ropy hair. He reveals also his fondness for fresh gay color and pervasive ornamental detail. Here, as in most of his works, Giovanni renounces solemnity and force in favor of delicacy and charm.

Although the name of the painter of "The Annunciation" in *Plate III* is not known definitely, he was clearly influenced by the work of Fra Filippo Lippi and may indeed have worked under him. The charm of this painting springs from its great simplicity and delicate coloring.

Plates IV and IVa are delightful details from two cassone panels which recount in continuous style Jason's conquest of the Golden Fleece and connected incidents in the famous Greek legend of the Argonauts. The panels were painted by two different followers, perhaps studio helpers, of Pesellino.

The meticulously painted "Portrait of a Young Man" (*Plate V*) was for many years thought to be the work of Antonello da Messina who worked in Venice in 1475. However, its many points of similarity to portraits by Giovanni Bellini have led scholars to the conclusion that it was painted by him and not by Antonello.

It has been suggested that Tura's famous tondo "The Flight into Egypt," (*Plate VI*), together with its companion pieces, "The Adoration of the Magi" in the Fogg Museum and "The Circumcision" in the Gardner Museum, at one time decorated a baptismal font, but it seems far more probable that they were the central predella panels of a large altarpiece such as the Roverella altarpiece formerly in San Giorgio fuori le Mura in Ferrara.

Still uncertain as to authorship is *Plate VII* and its subject is also questioned. The boy has the features of the Este family and has been called Borso d'Este and Ercole d'Este. Judging from the costume, however, which indicates a date of approximately 1470, and from the apparent age of the boy, it seems more likely that he is some younger member of the Este family, born about 1455. The attribution of the portrait to Tura in the light of available facts and expert study appears to be the most acceptable one.

Crivelli's delight in decorative detail is clearly revealed in his painting of "The Madonna and Child" (*Plate VIII*). He has drawn the figures and their richly elegant accessories with loving care and has blended his colors into a most harmonious composition. Attributed to Fra Carnevale is the exquisite "The Birth of the Virgin" of which a detail is shown in *Plate IX*. The foreground is sparingly occupied by ladies moving to and fro with quiet dignity. The significant scene, however, takes place far away within a stately loggia, or open room, of a palace. At the far end of the room an open cupboard reveals familiar household objects, while at the left, in a porch, are smart young men returned from hunting with hounds and falcons. Beyond is a street with men and horses, then the dark, dancing sea with little ships under sail. Over all is the blue sky lively with flying geese and delicate clouds that frolic like dolphins. The delightfulness of the architectural setting is greatly enhanced by the amazingly fine condition of the painting. The limpid delicacy of the colors and the smoothness of the glazed surface are beautifully preserved.

Portrayed in *Plate X* is a most appealing characterization of the wealthy Florentine merchant Francesco Sassetti (1421-1490) and his son, Teodoro. Recent research into the history of the Sassetti family by Florence de Roover and others identifies the boy as Francesco's eldest son who was born in 1460 and not, as was formerly supposed, the youngest, also named Teodoro, who was born shortly after his brother's death in 1479. This places the painting among Ghirlandaio's earliest work, giving new evidence of the development of this great fifteenth century painter's style.

A detail of Vittore Carpaccio's "The Meditation on the Passion" was chosen for *Plate XI*. In the full painting at the museum can be seen the dead Christ, seated upon a throne in the center between Saint Jerome and Job. The key to the interpretation is provided by the distorted Hebrew characters on the stone block on which Job is sitting and in which scholars have deciphered the phrase "that my Redeemer liveth" and the number 19, referring to the nineteenth chapter of the Book of Job, where those words appear. The two sages, who by their experiences and writings, announced the Resurrection and its meaning in human life, sit here together meditating upon the Passion of Christ. The detail in this book, taken from the lower left hand corner, is of Saint Jerome.

"The Adoration of the Shepherds" (*Plate XII*) by Andrea Mantegna is a superb example of this fifteenth century Italian painter's work. Architectural form was a consuming interest to Mantegna from first to last. It was applied not only to the buildings which frequent his pictures but to all the elements which play a part in his designs. Trees, rocks, draperies, and even human figures took on the grandeur and finality of architecture to an extent that has not been paralleled in the work of any other artist. This is not to say that Mantegna's portrayals of people and other living things are inanimate, but rather that they are clothed in eternal forms.

The great Venetian painter, Titian, is represented by a delightful early work. In this "Madonna and Child" (*Plate XIII*) he has used one of his favorite backgrounds, half dark curtain and half landscape, to silhouette the figure of the Virgin holding the infant Christ tenderly on her lap.

In *Plate XIV*, the fine "Portrait of a Young Man" by Bronzino is very possibly one of the Dukes of Urbino. Presuming this to be so, it is most likely Guidobaldo II (1514-1574).

"The Angel of the Annunciation," reproduced in *Plate XV*, is of approximately the same period as Giovanni di Paolo's "The Presentation in the Temple" (*Plate II*). The contrast in style between the Sienese and French painters is interestingly marked and this picture from Picardy makes an appropriate transition from the Italian Renaissance paintings selected for this book to the early Flemish works. "The Angel of the Annunciation" decorated the reverse side of the wing of a dismembered altarpiece, and was balanced when the altarpiece was closed by the Virgin Annunciate on the opposite wing. The painter was undoubtedly influenced by Roger van der Weyden, and the date 1451 which appears on the sill of the porch in which the archangel kneels, shows that the painting was made during Roger's lifetime.

One of the greatest Flemish painters was Hubert Van Eyck. "The Crucifixion," of which a detail is shown in *Plate XVI*, is an oil painting transferred from wood onto canvas. It is a human scene of surpassing richness and variety. Before a majestic and dispassionate mountain landscape, a crowd is gathered, showing in the attitudes, and on the faces, indifference, curiosity, and hatred, side by side with gentleness, poignant tenderness and rending grief.

One of the best loved painters of the early sixteenth century is the Fleming, Gerard David. The lovely "Nativity" shown in *Plate XVII* (also in a detail) is the central panel of an altarpiece. The modest and dignified figures, the tenderly watchful beasts, and the reverence of the angel choir illustrate well David's characteristic union of simplicity with grace.

The rare and fascinating masterpiece "The Adoration of the Magi" (*Plate XVIII*) has the distinction of being the one and only work by Joos van Wassenhove (Joos van Gent) in America. It must have been painted in or about 1467. The picture, which is rather large, is painted in the medium of tempera on fine canvas, instead of in oil on gesso-coated wood as was the general rule in fifteenth-century Flanders. Thus the texture of the paint is mat, which gives to the work an effect of reticence and understatement that serves to enhance the picture's expression of mediaeval remoteness. The climax of the scene, shown in the detail reproduced, centers around the highbred Virgin holding her frail Child while the grave old king bows in adoration. The picture also shows a spacious room in which Joseph bends toward the Virgin at the right and the two younger kings are seen standing at the left. A group of reverent country folk crowd together outside the porch. Another gem is Joos van Cleve's "Annunciation," a detail of which was taken for *Plate XIX*. The painting admirably displays Joos' delight and skill in depicting finely appointed interiors.

One of the most superb draughtsmen and painters of portraits was Hans Holbein, the Younger, particularly noted for his renderings of the English nobility of his time. The portrait of "Lady Lee" was done during his last period. It could not be said that he flattered her, for he gave her a sharp, rather shrewish look. On the other hand he must have pleased her by his meticulous attention to the details of her modish costume. The second example of Holbein's work is "Edward VI, when Prince of Wales." The short-lived Edward was born at Hampton Court on October 12th, 1537, the son of Henry VIII by his third queen, Jane Seymour. The charming boyish subject and the gay coloring make it one of Holbein's popular works. The third Holbein, "Benedikt von Hertenstein" (*Plate XXII*), bears the inscription on the wall: DA. ICH. HET. DIE. GESTALT. WAS. ICH. 22. JAR. ALT. 1517. H. H: PINGEBAT, and may be translated, "When I looked like this I was 22 years old. 1517. Painted by H. H." This painting, illustrating Holbein's early style, was done in oils on paper which was later mounted on a panel.

The life of the Flemish peasant is the undivided theme of Bruegel's later pictures, and the background of landscape assumes an importance hitherto unessayed. His style becomes grander and the figures that before had crowded his panels, sometimes to the point of bewilderment, are reduced to a reasonable number. "The Harvesters" (*Plate XXIII*) bears the signature Bruegel and the date L X V (denoting 1565). It is one of five pictures by Bruegel which symbolize the months of the year, mentioned in 1669 in the inventory of Archduke Leopold William, Governor General of the Netherlands. Bruegel's lusty peasants at work, at rest or indulging in gargantuan meals or frolicking festivities, have never enjoyed more popular attention than they do today. With satire like that of Rabelais, the artist shows in the detail (*Plate XXIV*) how the hungry people in the foreground cram food into mouths already full, or drink with great gulps from crocks or stoups.

Metsu epitomizes the seventeenth century Dutch painter's taste for strong but decorative architecture, rich fabrics and rugs, and gleaming basins and ewers that brighten shadowy interiors with their reflected light. But it is the conscious well-being emanating from the gracious and pleasant mannered household that makes "A Visit to the Nursery" a particularly good example of the kind of genre that Metsu, like his contemporaries Terborch, de Hooch, and Vermeer, often chose to paint—the genre of well-to-do contentment. *Plate XXIVa* is a detail of one of the figures in this pleasant domestic scene.

One of the most prolific artists is the Flemish painter Rubens, represented in *Plate XXV* by a detail of "The Triumphal Entry of Henry IV into Paris." As the triumphant procession surges onward we see Henry high above the turmoil, riding alone in a golden quadriga with white horses. His proud head is bare, and he wears a suit of shining armor. One hand grasps the rim of the chariot while the other carries a branch of olive. Victory, flying through the air, places a wreath of laurel on his head, while the helmeted goddess Bellona holds the reins, and Apollo, crowned with laurel, follows with his harp.

Between the main groups of Flemish and Dutch paintings in this selection of color prints is a highly picturesque painting by an unknown British artist of approximately the same period as Rubens. *Plate XXVI* is a detail of a large canvas entitled "Henry Frederick, Prince of Wales, and Sir John Harington." Henry Frederick Stuart (1594-1612) was the eldest son of James I, King of England. The double portrait was painted, as the inscription shows, in 1603, when the prince was nine and his friend eleven years old. The artist has shown Henry sheathing his sword after giving the *coup de grâce* to the stag, whose antlers are held by young Harington. Both are dressed in hunting clothes closely resembling the armor of the time.

The renowned Dutch painter, Frans Hals, not only interests us by his frank observation of character, but also reassures us by the solidity and simplicity of his forms and refreshes us by the brilliance and variety he achieved with the use of a comparatively restricted palette. His

"Portrait of a Woman" (*Plate XXVII*) is typical of Hals in its technical adroitness, but the characterization of the sitter is exceptionally sensitive, perhaps merely because she was more thoughtful and refined than most of the women who sat for him. Architectural settings such as the one in this portrait are almost unknown in works by Hals.

Of a very different character from Hals was his contemporary Rembrandt who concerned himself more deeply with the spiritual side of life. Three subjects are grouped together (*Plates XXVIII, XXIX and XXX*). The first, "Man with a Magnifying Glass," is a detail of one of Rembrandt's magnificent later portraits, painted in the last decade of his life. The name of the interesting person it portrays has recently been discovered. On the basis of the striking likeness to an engraved self-portrait, he has been identified as Jan Lutma the Younger, a silversmith by profession, to which the magnifying glass in his hand bears witness. The second example, the life-size "Head of Christ," appears from its scale to be a fragment cut from a larger picture. But its expression of warmth and tenderness, especially in the dark thoughtful eyes, gives the painting adequate significance in its present form. Rembrandt was also interested in the subject of the disciples' recognition of their Lord at Emmaus, and his painting of Christ in the cloak of a wayfarer, his hands clasped on a pilgrim's staff, may represent the newly risen Christ as he appeared on the Emmaus road. This is a picture of Rembrandt's late period, dated 1661.

The character of the Dutch landscape is probably as well known through the medium of paintings as is the English countryside. One of the great Dutch landscape painters, Jacob van Ruisdael, is represented in *Plate XXXI* by a superb painting of "Wheatfields." But Ruisdael's pictures do not always represent actual localities; they are thoughtfully composed paintings, a studied synthesis of the quiet and charming features of his native land.

Vermeer's "Young Woman with a Water Jug" (*Plate XXXII*) is typical of the works of this rare master in the suspended activity of its subject—the simple composition, and the unsurpassed observation of the way indirect sunlight plays on the walls of a room and on the familiar objects within it. Vermeer's palette is cooler than that of his contemporary Terborch, and also Metsu, de Hooch, and Dou. His actors are generally less busily mundane than theirs, and his workmanship is broader, more daring, and at the same time more delicately accurate.

Admirers of Vermeer love to pick out the objects repeated in his paintings—the lion-headed chair, the little white Delft jug, the painting of Cupid holding up a letter, of which we see only the corner in "A Girl Asleep" (*Plate XXXIII*), and the rumpled rug. Yet it isn't these things, or even the signature, that stamp the painting as a true Vermeer, but the enveloping atmosphere, the tranquility and the strange timelessness.

A less known Dutch painter is Willem van de Velde, the Younger, and his "Entrance to a Dutch Port" (*Plate XXXIV*), while laying little claim to greatness, is a pleasing enough painting in its own quiet way. These big three-masted seagoing ships, the smaller fishing boats, and the laden fisherman with his young helper wading up the sandy beach, combine to record for us the maritime trade that made seventeenth century Holland prosperous.

Perhaps the greatest of all Spanish painters is El Greco. Though born on the small Greek island of Crete and studying and working in Italy during the earlier part of his life, the paintings he has left to posterity seem entirely Spanish in feeling. The painting of "Cardinal Don Fernando Niño de Guevara" (*Plate XXXV*), an archbishop and an officer of the Grand Inquisition, is an extraordinary example of El Greco's portraiture. This work originally hung opposite Guevara's tomb in the Convento de San Pablo Ermitaño in Toledo. In *Plate XXXVI* we find Greco's turbulent emotions most strikingly manifested. The eerie lighting and the strangely elongated figures in this "Adoration of the Shepherds" is characteristic of the painter's highly individual style. Another violently imaginative example of his genius is to be found in the unique "View of Toledo" (*Plate XXXVII*). In this superb painting, El Greco has sacrificed the actual arrangement of the city's buildings to the dramatic effect. The view is taken from across the Tagus, showing the castle of San Servando and the bridge called Alcántara in the foreground. The cathedral and the Alcázar may be distinguished at the crest of the city. This is the only landscape known to have been painted by El Greco.

Velazquez, immortal painter of the Spanish Court, displays his consummate skill in the portrait of "Cardinal Gaspar de Borja y Velasco" (*Plate XXXVIII*). The entire expression is that of an alert, narrow, obstinate, courageous, and withal highly complex man; a man whose qualities one is bound to respect but whose ends are perhaps achieved in ways that leave us more astonished than enthusiastic. This baffling impression of a "difficult" and rather dangerous personality is amply borne out by what we know of the sitter. In a council of state, convened to consider what action should be taken to put down an uprising (in Catalonia in 1640) Borja declared, "As a conflagration can be quenched only by much water, so the fire of disloyalty and revolt can be quelled only by rivers of blood."

Probably Velazquez's earliest existing portrait of "King Philip IV, of Spain" is reproduced in *Plate XXXIX*. The painting was purchased from Velazquez by Doña Antonia de Ypeñarrieta, who married Diego del Corral in 1627. Until it was acquired for the Altman collection, the picture remained in the possession of the Corral family. The Metropolitan Museum has the receipt, dated December 4, 1624, in which Velazquez acknowledges receiving from Doña Antonia 800 *reales* in part payment for three pictures—this portrait of Philip, one of Olivares, and one, now lost, of García Pérez.

The harmonious arrangement of Murillo's "Virgin and Child" is enhanced by the simplicity of the composition and the sobriety and dignity of the Virgin's face and figure. Her calm repose is charmingly contrasted with the lively posture of the Child, a detail of which is shown in *Plate XL*. There is vitality in every inch of him, in his sturdy body, his rosy flesh, his bright eyes, his crisply curling hair—it seems even to animate the scarf which is twisted and swirled about him. *Plate XLI* reproduces the entire picture of the Santiago "Virgin and Child," so named from the collection in which it was for centuries. In this painting there is no sign of Murillo's famous vaporous manner; the figures are solidly built and have no tendency to melt into the background. But despite their realism they are freely and largely constructed with an almost careless competence. Such apparent simplicity, such ease, are the height of dexterity and reveal the artist in the ripeness of his development.

Delightful and skillful paintings of animals are often to be found in paintings by the old masters. The detail of a little dog (*Plate XLa*) was taken from Mazo's full-length portrait of Philip IV's small daughter "The Infanta Maria Teresa." Maria Teresa later became Queen of France, the long-suffering wife of the Sun King, Louis XIV. The painter, Mazo, was born about 1612 and was married in his early twenties to Velazquez's daughter Francisca. When the great artist died in 1660, Mazo became court painter and held the post until his own death in 1667.

So well known is Don Manuel Osorio with his pet magpie (*Plate XLII*) that no introduction is necessary. Goya probably painted him when he was about three years old, in 1787, the same year in which his father, the Count of Altamira, is known to have been painted by Goya.

The French paintings of the 18th Century included in this selection are headed by François Boucher's "Dispatch of the Messenger" (*Plate XLIII*). A group of four pastorals of which this was one formed, according to the critic Diderot, *un petit poème charmant* in the Salon of 1765. They showed the shepherd sending a message to his love by carrier pigeon; the shepherdess receiving it; the shepherdess and a friend sharing its contents and planning a rendezvous; and finally the happy meeting of the lovers. In no way dissimilar in point of view is Fragonard's "The Billet Doux" (*Plate XLIV*) which also typifies the perfumed daintiness of a bygone Parisian society. "The Billet Doux" is dashing to a breath-taking degree and is, at the same time, one of the most delicate of Fragonard's works. The happy young lady slipping a love letter into a bouquet of flowers has been identified as Boucher's youngest daughter, Marie Émilie, who in 1773 married the architect Cuvillier. His name is decipherable on the letter.

Antoine Watteau, a forerunner of both Boucher and Fragonard, was probably the most poetic of all French painters. Early in his career his interest in the theatre resulted in many drawings and paintings of actors of all types. The painting of "The French Comedians" (*Plate XLV*) came originally from the collection of Watteau's great patron Jean de Jullienne, and belonged at one time to Frederick the Great and the Prussian royal family. In it Watteau has painted some of the typical characters of the theatre of his time, giving to several of them the features of famous contemporary French actors.

The portrait of "Mlle. Charlotte du Val d'Ognes" (*Plate XLVI*) was painted during the Directoire, and the austere taste of the time is reflected in the simple arrangement. The young lady is looking up from her drawing portfolio; the window in front of which she sits makes a rim of light about her, and reflections from her paper and the blank wall round about light up all the figure so that no detail is lost. Jacques Louis David was cold and impersonal in his subject pictures, but his portraits are quite different. In this case he was moved strongly by the charm of the sitter and on that account the work has a lasting appeal that his great classical subjects lack.

The British school of painting is perhaps best known for its portraits of the fashionable London society of the 18th century and for renderings of the peaceful countryside. One of the best known portrait painters of the time was Sir Joshua Reynolds, whose "Lady Smith and her Children" is shown in *Plate XLVII*. Reynolds' account book shows several entries during the year 1787 of amounts totaling 310 pounds paid by Sir Robert Smith for "Lady Smith and Three Children" and a "Fancy Child."

Unique in the annals of painting is William Blake, for his style does not fit in with the accepted school of any period, far less that of 18th Century England. His illustration of the New Testament parable of "The Wise and Foolish Virgins" is reproduced in *Plate XLVIII*. Here, at dawn, the angel has come to proclaim the arrival of the Bridegroom. The five wise virgins, radiant in the light of their lamps, are sharply contrasted with the heedless, who are lost in the darkness of their own folly. This watercolor is one of Blake's four versions of the same subject.

Although Mrs. Calmady felt the family could not afford to pay for a portrait, on the advice of an artist her children were presented to Sir Thomas Lawrence, who was so captivated by them that he reduced his usual fee of two hundred and fifty guineas to one hundred and fifty pounds, and wanted to start work at once. When the final painting was done (*Plate XLIX*), Lawrence is said to have declared: "This is my best picture. I have no hesitation in saying so— my best picture of the kind, quite . . . one of the few I should wish hereafter to be known by."

The final selection from the British school of painting is the charming "Old Bridge" by Frederick W. Watts (*Plate L*). This painting was once attributed to Constable of whom Watts himself was a very able follower.

Influenced by the British school, the nineteenth century American painter Thomas Sully is well known for his innumerable gracious portraits. His romantic painting "Mother and Son" (*Plate LI*) represents the painter's daughter Jane Sully Darley, the wife of William H. W. Darley and her small son Francis Thomas Sully Darley. The work bears the date of 1840. Thomas Sully is followed by his contemporary, George Inness, whose painting "Peace and Plenty" (*Plate LII*) is one of the most reproduced paintings in the Museum's collection. Inness painted this canvas in 1865 from sketches made at Medfield, Massachusetts. In his productions of this period, Inness still followed the tenets of the Hudson River School and it is he who reaches its highest achievement with this noble painting.

Another leading name in American art is Thomas Eakins who was still active after the turn of this century. "Max Schmitt in a Single Scull" (*Plate LIII*) is signed with a remarkable and inimitable signature—a miniature portrait of the artist himself, seen rowing at good speed and in excellent form (he too was a trained oarsman) in the middle distance. On the stern of his boat appear the name EAKINS and the date 1871.

The remaining paintings in the book are French. After Daumier and Courbet come the painters of the later nineteenth century who have made an indelible mark upon the history of art. Breaking away from traditions, Cézanne and his contemporary revolutionaries laid the cornerstone of modern painting. The Impressionists and Post-Impressionists created a style that separated them from their French predecessors as completely as the earlier French had been separated from the Renaissance painters of Italy or from the artists of Holland and Flanders. More in the technical tradition of their immediate predecessors are Daumier and Courbet. Daumier made his living by drawing for the press, but found time to record his epoch in a few paintings of profound insight and power. His masterly draughtsmanship, the solidity of his figures, and his racy comment on life are all to be found in his splendid "Third Class Carriage," reproduced in *Plate LIV*. Despite his blunt revolt against tradition, Courbet painted with less social significance. "Lady in a Riding Habit," shown in *Plate LV*, is an excellent example of Courbet's work. The dark forest and stormy sky make an effective romantic setting for this simple portrait.

Unlike the Impressionists Pissarro, Monet and Sisley, Manet's interest in landscape was always secondary to his interest in figures. Although in "Boating" (*Plate LVI*), he has adopted the new theories of light, he has used the brilliant water simply as a setting for the man and woman sitting in the boat. This painting was made in the Summer of 1874 at the French town of Argenteuil where Manet spent some time with Claude Monet painting *en pleine air*.

Cézanne, inherent experimentalist and popularly termed father of modern painting, is represented in *Plate LVII* by "The Gulf of Marseilles Seen from L'Estaque." Cézanne often painted at l'Estaque and this attractive view of the red-roofed town sloping down to the blue waters of the Mediterranean was painted about 1883.

Unsurpassed for his rendering of the ballet is Degas. The masterfully light touch and delicacy of feeling he has imparted to his drawings and paintings have gained for him a place amongst the masters of all time. In "Rehearsal of the Ballet on the Stage," Degas' interest in movement and his skill in presenting it reached its highest expression. Intensively trained physically for a very specific career, the ballet girls offered him movement at its most exquisite— nervous, swift, and nicely balanced, light and rhythmical as lyric poetry. In quite a different vein we find "Woman with Chrysanthemums" (*Plate LIX*). This painting of Mme. Hertel is one of Degas' finest portraits. Contrary to custom, the portrait is relegated to one side of the composition, the larger part of the canvas being occupied by a huge bouquet of chrysanthe-mums on a table. The flowers, painted with precision and charm, form an exquisite arrange-ment of color; the portrait is a masterpiece of penetrating understanding and sympathy.

One of the finest Renoirs in the museum's collection is "By the Seashore" reproduced in *Plate LX*. Like Watteau and Fragonard, Renoir carried on the tradition of celebrating the beauty and charm of the French woman, but he embodied her piquant fragrance in a nine-teenth century form that clearly distinguishes it from its predecessors. Renoir, unlike most of the French painters of his day, lived to see wide acclaim of his work.

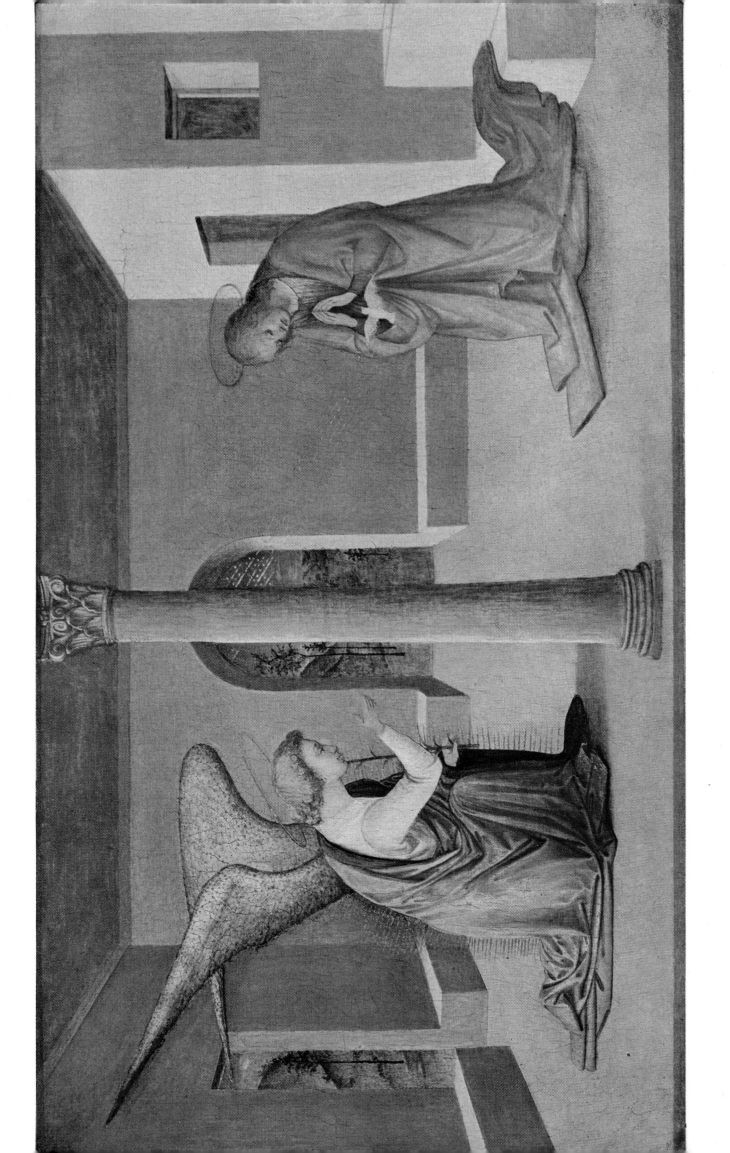

Plate IV
A FOLLOWER OF PESELLINO
ITALIAN, ABOUT 1422-1457
DETAIL FROM A CASSONE PANEL REPRESENTING
THE STORY OF THE ARGONAUTS
Gift of J. Pierpont Morgan

Plate IVa
A FOLLOWER OF PESELLINO
ITALIAN, ABOUT 1422-1457
DETAIL FROM A CASSONE PANEL REPRESENTING
THE STORY OF THE ARGONAUTS
Gift of J. Pierpont Morgan

Plate IX
FRA CARNEVALE (?)
ITALIAN, ACTIVE BY 1456—DIED 1484
THE BIRTH OF THE VIRGIN (Detail)
Rogers and Gwynne M. Andrews Funds

Plate XI
VITTORE CARPACCIO
VENETIAN, ABOUT 1455—DIED BETWEEN 1525-1526
MEDITATION ON THE PASSION (Detail)
Kennedy Fund

Plate XII
ANDREA MANTEGNA
ITALIAN, 1431-1506
THE ADORATION OF THE SHEPHERDS
Anonymous Gift

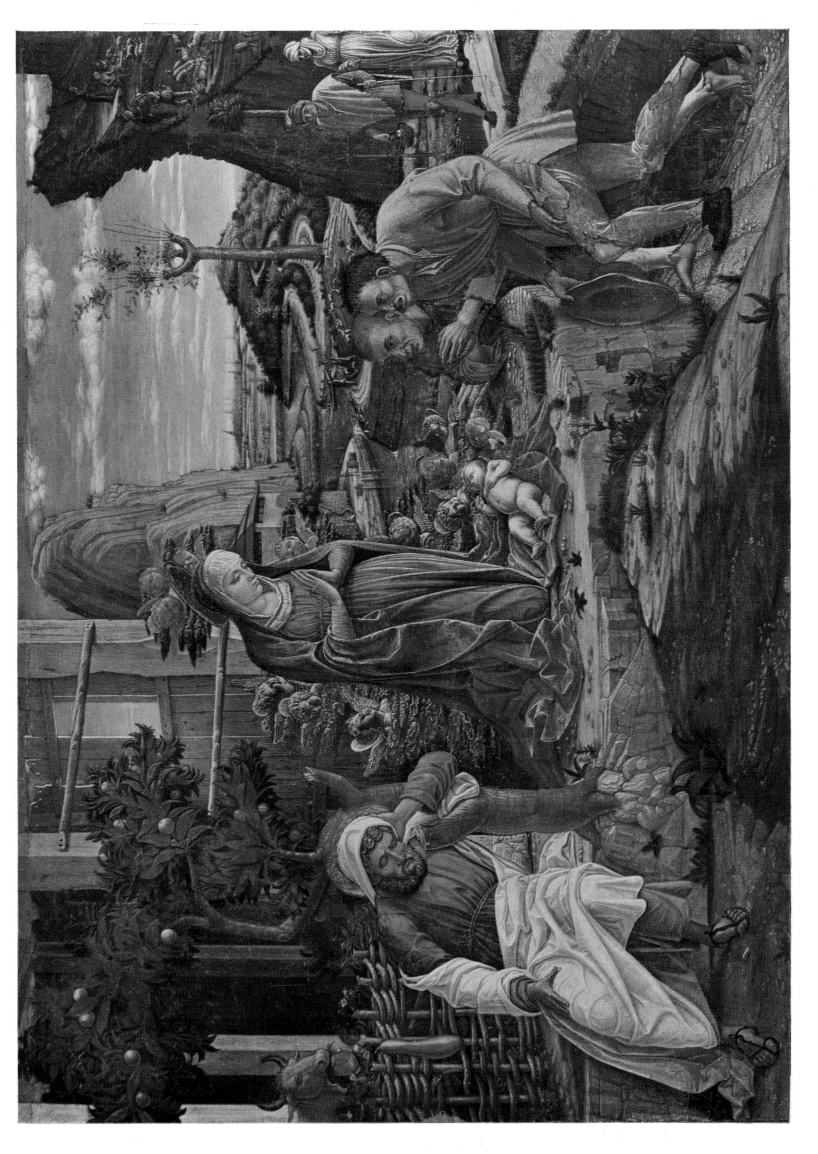

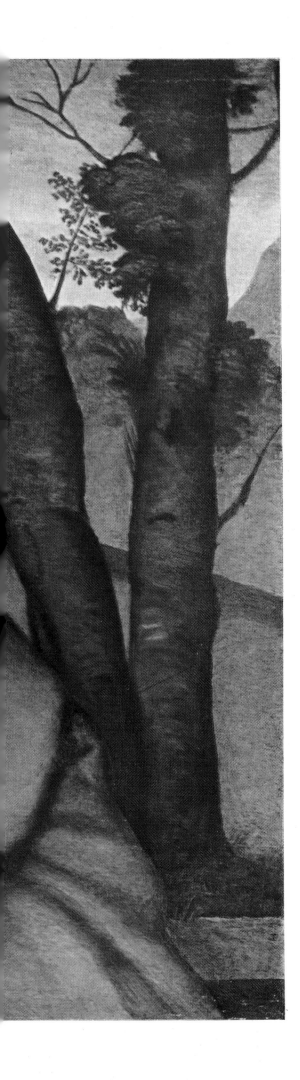

Plate XIII
TITIAN
ITALIAN, 1477(?)-1576
THE MADONNA AND CHILD
Jules S. Bache Collection

Plate XV
UNKNOWN FRENCH PAINTER
DATED 1451
THE ANGEL OF THE ANNUNCIATION
The Michael Friedsam Collection

Plate XXIV
PIETER BRUEGEL, THE ELDER
FLEMISH, ACTIVE 1551—DIED 1569
THE HARVESTERS (Detail)
Rogers Fund

Plate XXIVa
GABRIEL METSU
DUTCH, 1629-1667
A VISIT TO THE NURSERY (Detail)
Gift of J. Pierpont Morgan

Plate XXVII
FRANS HALS
DUTCH, AFTER 1580-1666
PORTRAIT OF A WOMAN
Gift of Henry G. Marquand

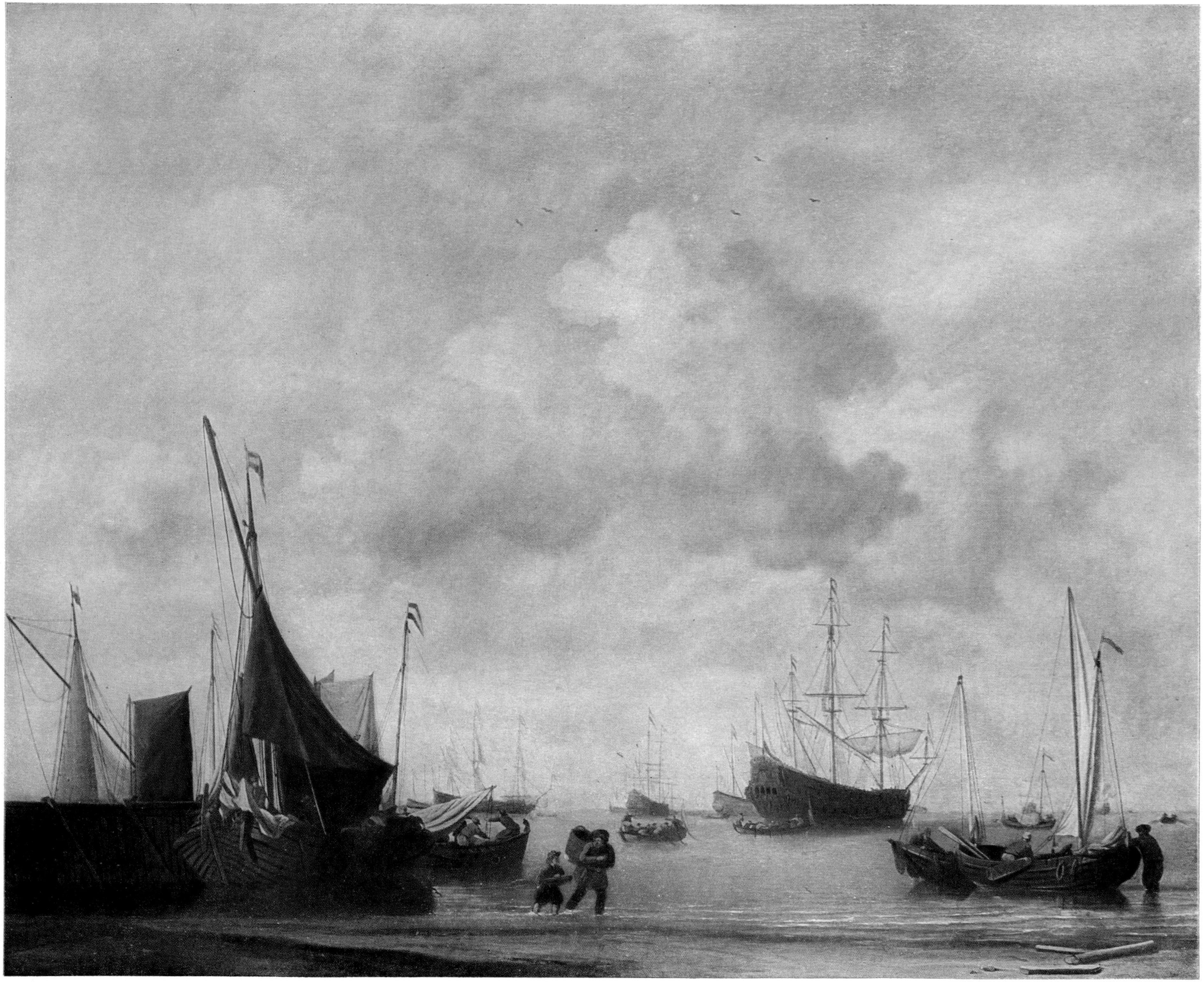

Plate XXXV
EL GRECO
SPANISH, 1541-1614
CARDINAL DON FERNANDO NIÑO DE GUEVARA
Bequest of Mrs. H. O. Havemeyer

Plate XL
BARTOLOMÉ ESTEBAN MURILLO
SPANISH, 1618-1682
VIRGIN AND CHILD (Detail)
Rogers Fund

Plate XLa
JUAN BAUTISTA MARTÍNEZ DEL MAZO
SPANISH, ABOUT 1612-1667
THE INFANTA MARIA TERESA
Rogers Fund

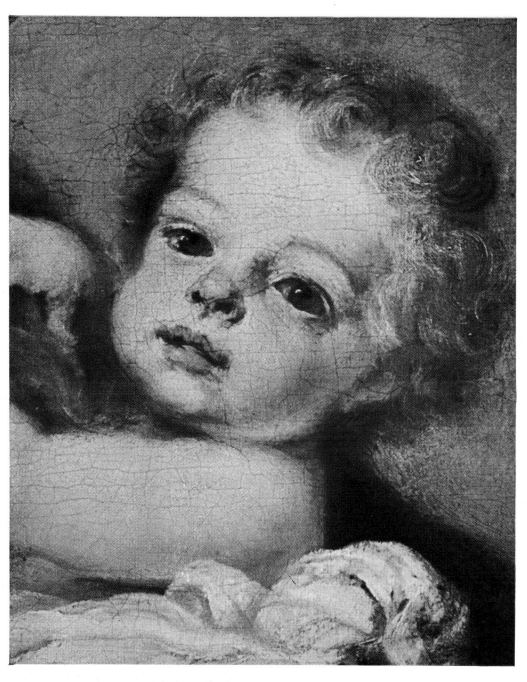

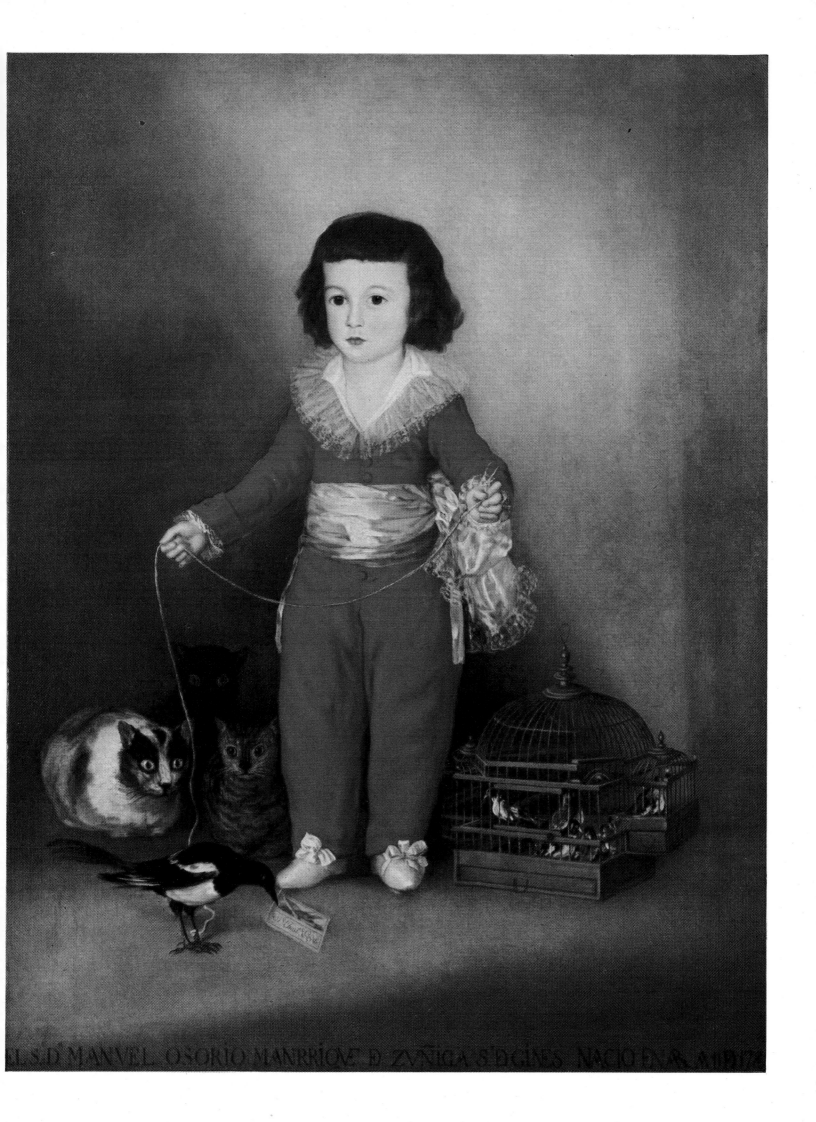

Plate XLV
JEAN-ANTOINE WATTEAU
FRENCH, 1684-1721
THE FRENCH COMEDIANS
Jules S. Bache Collection

Plate LIV
HONORÉ DAUMIER
FRENCH, 1808-1879
THE THIRD CLASS CARRIAGE
Bequest of Mrs. H. O. Havemeyer

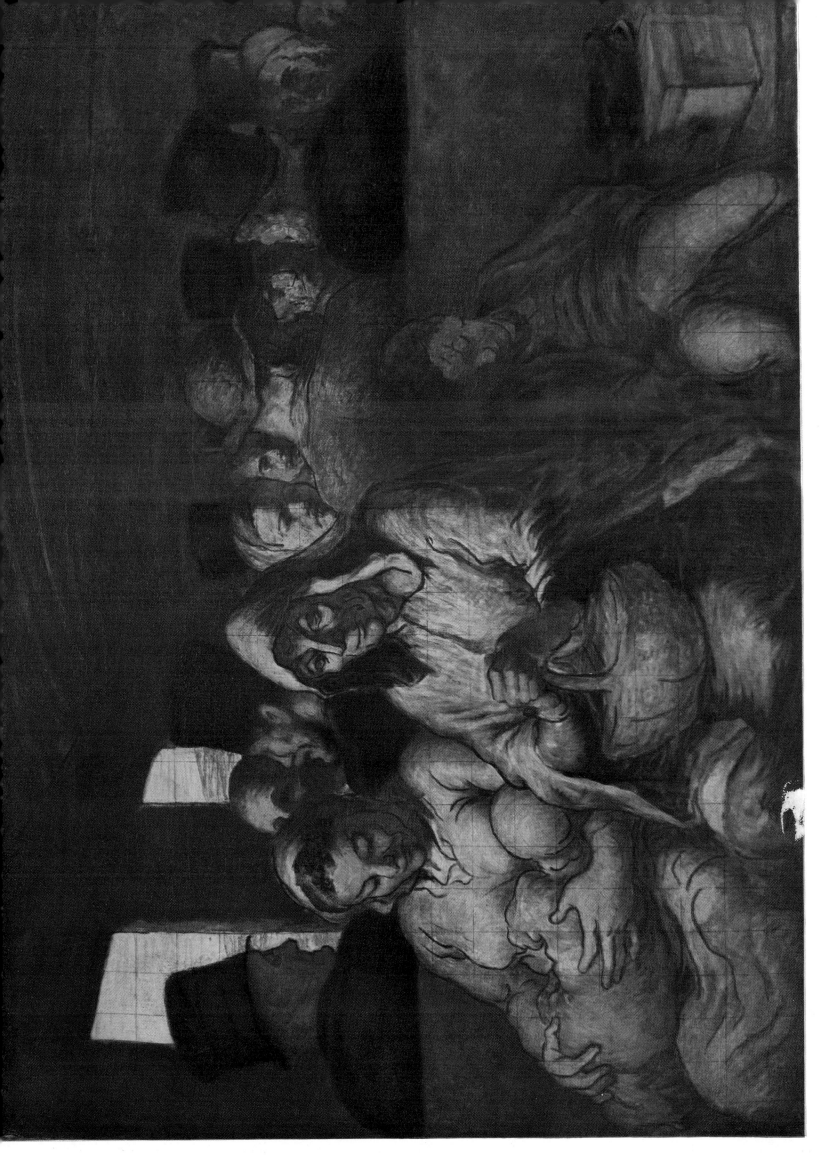

Plate LVIII
EDGAR HILAIRE GERMAINE DEGAS
FRENCH, 1834-1917
REHEARSAL OF THE BALLET ON THE STAGE
Gift of Horace Havemeyer